"The battle we wage is not for ourselves alone, but for all true Americans."

—MANIFESTO OF THE NIAGARA MOVEMENT, 1905

THE NAACP:
AN ORGANIZATION WORKING TO END DISCRIMINATION

BY ANDREW SANTELLA

Content Reviewer: Sheila Douglas, Senior Media Relations Specialist, NAACP

The Child's World®

Published in the United States of America by The Child's World®
PO Box 326
Chanhassen, MN 55317-0326
800-599-READ
www.childsworld.com

The Child's World®: Mary Berendes, Publishing Director
Editorial Directions, Inc.: E. Russell Primm and Emily Dolbear, Editors; Katie Marsico and
Elizabeth K. Martin, Editorial Assistants; Dawn Friedman, Photo Researcher; Linda S. Koutris,
Photo Selector; Kerry Reid, Fact Researcher; Susan Hindman, Copy Editor; Lucia Raatma,
Proofreader; Tim Griffin/IndexServ, Indexer; Vicki Fischman, Page Production

Cover photograph: A large group at the Sixth Annual Youth Conference of the NAACP/© Corbis

Interior photographs ©: AP/Wide World Photos: 22, 28; Peter A. Harris/AP/Wide World Photos: 32; Lou
Krasky/AP/Wide World Photos: 35; Corbis: 2, 7, 9, 13, 19, 29; Bettmann/Corbis: 11, 17, 21, 25, 26, 27, 31;
Underwood & Underwood/Corbis: 15; AFP/Corbis: 33; The Granger Collection, New York: 6; Hulton
Archive/Getty Images: 16, 30; Illinois State Historical Library: 12; Library of Congress: 8, 14, 18, 20, 23.

Library of Congress Cataloging-in-Publication Data
Santella, Andrew.
The NAACP : an organization working to end discrimination / by Andrew Santella
p. cm. — (Journey to freedom)
"An editorial directions book"—T.p. verso.
Includes bibliographical references and index.
Contents: The birth of the NAACP—The fight against lynching—The NAACP in the courts—The Civil Rights
Movement—New directions—Timeline.
ISBN 1-56766-540-3 (Library Bound : alk. paper)
1. National Association for the Advancement of Colored People—Juvenile literature. 2. National Association
for the Advancement of Colored People—History—Juvenile literature. 3. African Americans—Civil rights—
History—20th century—Juvenile literature. 4. Civil rights movements—United States—History—20th
century—Juvenile literature. 5. United States–Race relations—Juvenile literature. [1. National Association
for the Advancement of Colored People . 2. African Americans—Civil rights. 3. Civil rights movements.
4. Race relations.] I. Title. II. Series.
E185.5.N276S26 2003
323.1'196073'006073–dc21
2003004298

Contents

THIS BRAVE GROUP OF AFRICAN-AMERICANS WAS CALLED THE NIAGARA MOVEMENT. THE MEMBERS NAMED THEMSELVES AFTER NIAGARA FALLS, WHICH WERE CLOSE TO THEIR MEETING PLACE IN FORT ERIE, ONTARIO.

The Niagara Movement

In the summer of 1905, a group of 29 young **African-Americans** crossed the Niagara River into Canada. Their goal was to form an organization that would demand equal rights for African-Americans. They had come from all over the United States, and their plan was to meet in Buffalo, New York. However, they were not able to find a hotel that would accept them in Buffalo. So they met just across the river in the Canadian town of Fort Erie, Ontario. Their struggle to change America had to begin in another country.

They named their group the Niagara Movement, after nearby Niagara Falls. Their leader was a college professor named William Edward Burghardt (W. E. B.) Du Bois. He was well known for a book he had published in 1903 called *The Souls of Black Folks*. In his book, Du Bois had predicted that the greatest problem of the 20th century would be the color line that divided black and white people.

THE LEADER OF THE NIAGARA MOVEMENT WAS W. E. B. DuBois. HE WAS A WELL-KNOWN PROFESSOR AND AUTHOR.

For African-Americans, life at the start of the 20th century was filled with injustice. In many places, they were forced to attend second-rate schools for blacks only. African-Americans riding on trains often had to sit in sections reserved for "colored people." Even water fountains in public buildings were marked "white" and "colored." The practice of keeping African-Americans separate from white people was called **segregation.** It was widespread in the United States at the start of the 1900s.

AT ONE TIME, BLACKS AND WHITES WERE KEPT SEPARATE IN PUBLIC PLACES. SIMILAR RESTRICTIONS WERE ENFORCED FOR DRINKING FOUNTAINS, PARK BENCHES, AND AREAS IN RESTAURANTS.

Unfair laws kept many African-Americans from voting. Not a single black served in Congress. Black workers often earned less than white people in the same jobs. In many ways, they were treated like second-class citizens. Du Bois knew this had to end. "This nation will never stand **justified** before God until these things are changed," he wrote in the Niagara Movement's 1905 Declaration of Principles.

Du Bois and the other members of the Niagara Movement called for an end to segregation. They wanted equal access to public schools, fair treatment in the courts, and the chance to earn a good living. The Niagara Movement was the first group of African-Americans to demand equality. The members vowed to achieve their demands by "voting where we may vote . . . [by] hammering at the truth; by sacrifice and work."

FOR MANY YEARS, BLACK AND WHITE CHILDREN DID NOT GO TO SCHOOL TOGETHER. ONLY BLACK CHILDREN ATTENDED THIS SCHOOL.

Not all African-Americans were ready to accept the Niagara Movement. The group's demands brought them into conflict with the most influential African-American of the time—Booker T. Washington. He urged blacks to take a slower, more gradual path to equality. He encouraged them to advance themselves through hard work and self-education. Washington believed that only after blacks earned economic success would they win full equality.

Du Bois and the Niagara Movement rejected Washington's approach. They were ready to fight for equality right away. The members of the Niagara Movement started more than 30 branches around the country.

Even though the group always seemed to be short of money for its activities, Du Bois and others worked tirelessly for equality. It did not come quickly or easily, however.

This became clear on August 14, 1908. That day, tensions between blacks and whites in Springfield, Illinois, boiled over. A white mob gathered to attack two African-Americans being held in the Springfield jail. When the whites discovered that the men had been taken away for their own protection, they went on a **rampage.** Over the next two days, the mob burned down 40 African-American homes and destroyed more than 20 businesses. Two blacks were murdered. To escape the violence, about 2,000 African-Americans fled Springfield in terror.

BOOKER T. WASHINGTON (OPPOSITE) WAS AN IMPORTANT AFRICAN-AMERICAN LEADER. BUT HE FELT THAT THE NIAGARA MOVEMENT WAS TRYING TO BRING ABOUT CHANGE TOO QUICKLY.

The Birth of the NAACP

News of the Springfield **riots** spread across the nation. To many, the riots proved that something had to be done to end racial injustice. The members of the Niagara Movement condemned the actions of the Springfield mob. The riots also stirred white supporters of the Niagara Movement into action.

William English Walling, a white **activist** from the South, wrote a report of the riots for the newspaper *The Independent.* In the article, "Race War in the North," Walling wrote that whites must treat blacks as equals. He asked his readers, "What large and powerful body of citizens is ready to come to their aid?"

THIS BLACK-OWNED BARBER SHOP WAS DESTROYED DURING THE 1908 RIOTS IN SPRINGFIELD, ILLINOIS.

Mary White Ovington, a white activist and social worker, was inspired by his question. She wrote to Walling, and the two gathered a group of friends in a New York City apartment on February 12, 1909—the 100th anniversary of the birth of Abraham Lincoln. Like the members of the Niagara Movement, Ovington and her friends decided to form an organization to fight for the rights of African-Americans. They issued an invitation to a national meeting titled "The Call." Some 60 important Americans of all races, including social worker Jane Addams, signed "The Call." The group named itself the National Negro Committee, which later became known as the National Association for the Advancement of Colored People (NAACP).

MARY WHITE OVINGTON JOINED FORCES WITH OTHER ACTIVISTS TO FIGHT FOR THE RIGHTS OF AFRICAN-AMERICANS.

From the start, the NAACP was made up of whites and blacks. One of its most important members was W. E. B. Du Bois. Other members of the Niagara Movement followed Du Bois into the ranks of the NAACP. There, they found the financial support that they had been lacking in the Niagara Movement. Du Bois was busy teaching at Atlanta University, but he found time to help lead the NAACP as director of publicity and research. Walling served as chair of the group's executive committee. The NAACP's first president was a white lawyer from Boston named Moorfield Storey.

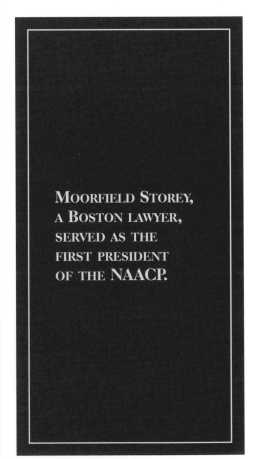

MOORFIELD STOREY, A BOSTON LAWYER, SERVED AS THE FIRST PRESIDENT OF THE NAACP.

In 1910, Du Bois started the *Crisis*, a magazine to represent the views of the NAACP. Instead of using the *Crisis* to promote the NAACP, however, he used it to express his own ideas about the future of African-Americans. Sometimes, these ideas clashed with the opinions of other leaders, and he quickly came into conflict with them. But the NAACP leaders allowed Du Bois to speak for the organization as long as they agreed on basic issues. Du Bois offered a clear vision of what he believed the NAACP should be.

Du Bois convinced some of the world's leading writers and thinkers to write articles for the *Crisis*. Author Langston Hughes, poet Vachel Lindsay, and Indian leader Mohandas Gandhi were among those who contributed to the magazine. Du Bois continued to edit the *Crisis* until 1934. Eventually, his disagreements with NAACP leaders caused him to break away from the group. Du Bois continued to work for the rights of black people around the world until his death in 1963.

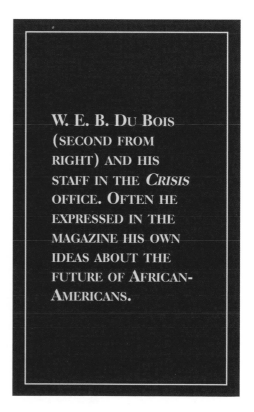

W. E. B. DU BOIS (SECOND FROM RIGHT) AND HIS STAFF IN THE *CRISIS* OFFICE. OFTEN HE EXPRESSED IN THE MAGAZINE HIS OWN IDEAS ABOUT THE FUTURE OF AFRICAN-AMERICANS.

The Fight against Lynching

From its start in 1909, the NAACP grew rapidly. The group established headquarters in New York City. In 1915, the NAACP led a **boycott** of *The Birth of a Nation,* a film about the Civil War and the rise of the **Ku Klux Klan.** The organization felt the movie portrayed African-Americans in a **racist** way. In 1917, the NAACP worked to change government rules so African-Americans could become officers in the military. By 1919, NAACP membership had grown to around 90,000. It had branch offices in more than 300 cities.

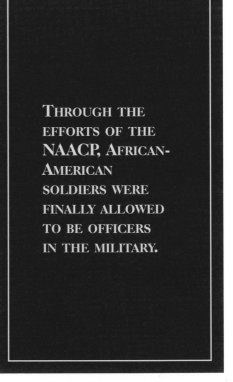

THROUGH THE EFFORTS OF THE NAACP, AFRICAN-AMERICAN SOLDIERS WERE FINALLY ALLOWED TO BE OFFICERS IN THE MILITARY.

The NAACP's greatest early battle was against **lynching.** Lynching is the taking of a person's life by mob violence. The lynching of African-Americans became an all-too-common practice in the United States in the 1880s and 1890s. Hundreds of African-Americans were killed in lynchings then. The practice continued into the 20th century. In 1919, some 70 African-Americans were lynched.

The NAACP took out advertisements in major newspapers demanding an end to lynching. The group convinced President Woodrow Wilson to make a public statement against lynching.

One of the leaders in the campaign against lynching was Ida B. Wells-Barnett, a founding member of the NAACP. She had long been involved in the struggle for **civil rights.** In the 1880s, she sued the Chesapeake and Ohio Railroad after she was forced to give up her seat and move to a blacks-only section of the train. Later, she was one of the founders of a newspaper in Memphis, Tennessee, called the *Free Speech and Headlight*—later called simply *Free Speech*.

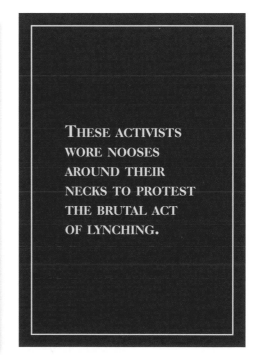

THESE ACTIVISTS WORE NOOSES AROUND THEIR NECKS TO PROTEST THE BRUTAL ACT OF LYNCHING.

After three of her friends were lynched, she began publishing articles describing the horrors of lynching. In response, mobs destroyed the offices of the *Free Speech*. Wells-Barnett moved to New York and then Chicago, and she continued her battle against lynching. She gave speeches all across the United States and in England. Her work helped stir worldwide action against this violent practice.

In 1919, the NAACP published a report called "30 Years of Lynching in the United States: 1889–1918." The report drew attention to the problem and increased public outcry against lynching. The NAACP's efforts eventually paid off. By the middle of the 20th century, lynching had ceased to be a widespread problem.

IDA B. WELLS-BARNETT WAS A STRONG VOICE FOR CIVIL RIGHTS. SHE SPOKE OUT AGAINST LYNCHING AND OTHER EXAMPLES OF INJUSTICE.

The NAACP in the Courts

For years, W. E. B. Du Bois was the only African-American among the NAACP's leaders. That changed in 1920. That year, James Weldon Johnson became the NAACP's first black executive secretary. He and his brother, Rosamond, wrote the song "Lift Every Voice and Sing," which became known as the "Negro National Anthem." Over the years, more and more African-Americans took on leading roles in the group.

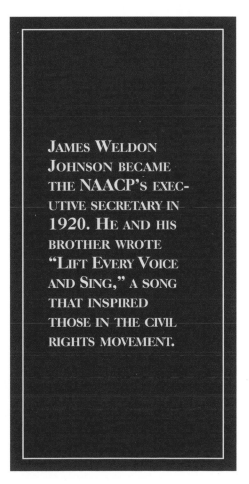

JAMES WELDON JOHNSON BECAME THE NAACP'S EXECUTIVE SECRETARY IN 1920. HE AND HIS BROTHER WROTE "LIFT EVERY VOICE AND SING," A SONG THAT INSPIRED THOSE IN THE CIVIL RIGHTS MOVEMENT.

As the organization grew, the NAACP tried a number of ways of bringing about change. Its leaders sought to influence the opinions of politicians and others in positions of power. They also fought to end unjust laws through the courts. In 1915, NAACP lawyers won their first legal battle. They challenged an Oklahoma law that made it difficult for African-Americans to vote in that state. The law required blacks to pass a test or pay a tax before they could vote. The NAACP argued that this law denied African-Americans their right to vote, as promised in the Constitution. The U.S. Supreme Court agreed. It ruled that the Oklahoma law violated the Constitution, and therefore it was not legal.

THE 1921 NAACP CONVENTION IN DETROIT. AS THE ORGANIZATION GREW, IT BECAME MORE POWERFUL AND TOOK ITS FIGHT TO AMERICA'S COURTS.

The NAACP continued to use the legal system to fight injustice. The organization worked to build a strong team of lawyers to fight and win court cases. In 1934, the NAACP hired Charles Hamilton Houston as its first **special counsel.** Houston was a professor, and later the dean, at Howard University Law School. He began building an outstanding legal team. Houston hired one of his former students, a young lawyer named Thurgood Marshall. Later, Marshall became the first African-American justice on the U.S. Supreme Court, serving from 1967 until 1991.

CHARLES HAMILTON HOUSTON WAS A PROFESSOR AT HOWARD UNIVERSITY LAW SCHOOL WHEN HE WAS HIRED BY THE NAACP AND SERVED AS SPECIAL COUNSEL.

Houston and his team attacked injustice in American education. In many places in the United States, African-Americans could not attend the same schools as white students. Some 17 states permitted such segregation. Courts had ruled that this segregation was legal—as long as African-Americans were given an education equal to that given to white students. This decision was known as the separate but equal rule. In fact, though, white schools often received more money and were usually more modern than black schools.

THROUGH THE WORK OF THE NAACP IN 1938, LLOYD GAINES GAINED ADMISSION TO THE UNIVERSITY OF MISSOURI LAW SCHOOL.

In 1935, Houston and Marshall won a legal battle to admit an African-American student to the University of Maryland. It was the first in a string of NAACP victories. In 1938, Houston won a similar case involving the University of Missouri law school. Over the next 20 years, NAACP lawyers took on school systems that shut out African-Americans.

In 1951, members of the NAACP branch in Topeka, Kansas, started a court case that changed the nation. The Reverend Oliver Brown and other parents of African-American children filed suit against the Topeka Board of Education. Their sons and daughters had been denied admission to white schools and had to travel long distances to get to one of Topeka's black schools. A U.S. district court ruled against Brown and the other parents. However, Marshall and the NAACP's legal team continued to fight through appeals to higher courts. The case came before the Supreme Court in 1953.

THURGOOD MARSHALL WENT ON TO BECOME THE FIRST AFRICAN-AMERICAN JUSTICE ON THE U.S. SUPREME COURT.

The Supreme Court combined the Brown case with similar cases from several other states. In deciding the cases in 1954, the court ruled that having separate public schools for white and black students was necessarily unfair. "Segregation of white and colored children in public schools has a detrimental [harmful] effect upon the colored children," wrote Chief Justice Earl Warren. "The **doctrine** of separate but equal has no place."

The case was a huge victory for African-Americans. However, the NAACP still had to work to make sure the court's decision was obeyed. Some political leaders in southern states refused to follow the court's ruling. They kept local schools closed to African-Americans. The NAACP appealed to President Dwight D. Eisenhower for help. In 1957, President Eisenhower ordered federal troops to Arkansas to force Governor Orval Faubus to open Little Rock's Central High School to African-Americans. The NAACP also led the battle to open the universities of Florida, Georgia, and Mississippi to blacks. Their victories helped give African-Americans equal opportunities for education.

THURGOOD MARSHALL (CENTER) STANDING WITH HIS COLLEAGUES AFTER THE SUPREME COURT'S HISTORIC RULING ON THE *BROWN V. THE BOARD OF EDUCATION* CASE IN **1954**

The Civil Rights Movement

In 1959, the NAACP celebrated its 50th anniversary. The group's membership had grown enormously. Its legal and political work had brought real change to the lives of African-Americans. A new generation of blacks was joining the fight for equality.

A minister from Atlanta, Georgia, named Martin Luther King Jr. was leading a new movement for civil rights. He urged ordinary African-Americans to take peaceful action to fight injustice. His followers organized protest marches and boycotts of businesses that **discriminated** against African-Americans.

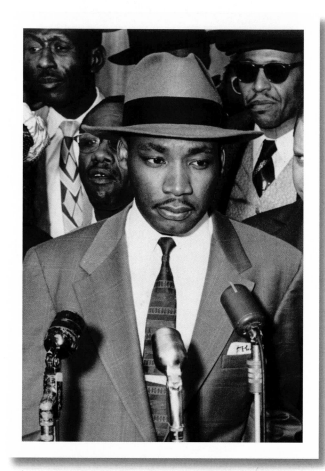

Martin Luther King Jr. was a minister from Atlanta, Georgia. He became a powerful force in the civil rights movement.

In 1955, Rosa Parks, an African-American secretary for the Montgomery, Alabama, branch of the NAACP, was arrested for refusing to give up her bus seat to a white rider. King responded by leading a yearlong boycott against the city's bus system. Montgomery's African-Americans refused to ride the buses until they were given the same treatment as whites. Thanks to the protest and an NAACP lawsuit, the Supreme Court made segregation on Alabama buses illegal.

ROSA PARKS (HERE WITH HER LAWYER) WAS ARRESTED FOR NOT GIVING UP HER SEAT ON A PUBLIC BUS. HER ACTION LED TO A BOYCOTT OF THE BUS SYSTEM IN MONTGOMERY, ALABAMA.

The civil rights movement of the 1950s and 1960s marked a whole new chapter in the fight for equality. The NAACP had made its mark by battling in the courts and in the political arena. Now, young people were taking to the streets to protest injustice peacefully. NAACP leaders made it clear that they did not approve of protests in which African-Americans might break laws.

However, NAACP members joined in some grass-roots protests. In 1960, members of the NAACP youth council in the South began protesting segregation at store lunch counters. They staged **sit-ins** at the lunch counters, refusing to move until they were served. The practice spread to other cities. As a result, more than 60 stores opened their lunch counters to African-Americans.

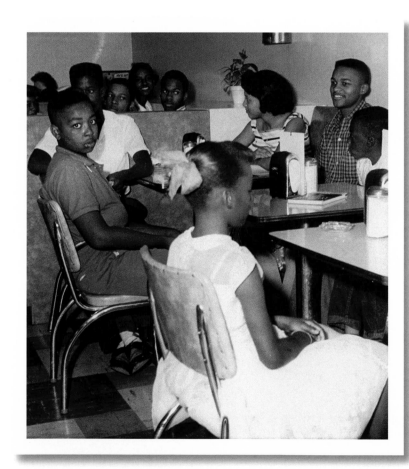

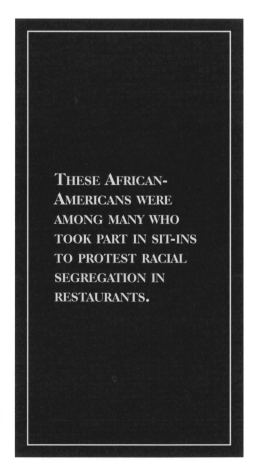

THESE AFRICAN-AMERICANS WERE AMONG MANY WHO TOOK PART IN SIT-INS TO PROTEST RACIAL SEGREGATION IN RESTAURANTS.

In 1963, the NAACP, led by Roy Wilkins, and other African-American groups organized a historic march in Washington, D.C. More than 250,000 people gathered at the Lincoln Memorial to demand civil rights for African-Americans. The protest showed the size and strength of the peaceful civil rights movement. The march sent a powerful message. The following year, Congress passed the Civil Rights Act of 1964. It outlawed discrimination in offices, schools, and public places.

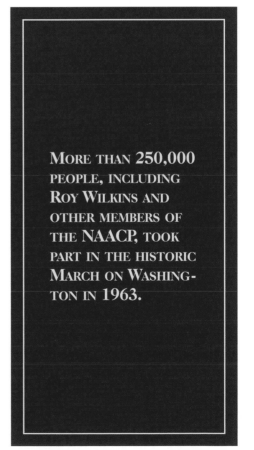

MORE THAN 250,000 PEOPLE, INCLUDING ROY WILKINS AND OTHER MEMBERS OF THE NAACP, TOOK PART IN THE HISTORIC MARCH ON WASHINGTON IN 1963.

However, the forces of injustice were not yet ready to give in. In 1963, an NAACP leader named Medgar Evers was murdered in front of his house in Jackson, Mississippi. At the same time, officials in Alabama and several other states were trying to ban NAACP activities. Again, the NAACP fought for its rights in court, and the U.S. Supreme Court ruled that states could not ban the organization.

The NAACP worked to build the political power of African-Americans in the South. For years, unfair voting rules had discouraged African-Americans from taking part in elections. NAACP efforts resulted in the passage of the Voting Rights Act of 1965. This led to more than 80,000 African-Americans registering to vote for the first time in Alabama, Arkansas, Mississippi, and South Carolina.

The NAACP did not work only through the courts. To honor African-American actors and actresses who did not receive recognition in the Hollywood entertainment industry, the NAACP established the Image Awards in 1968.

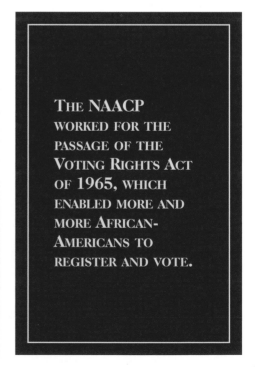

THE NAACP WORKED FOR THE PASSAGE OF THE VOTING RIGHTS ACT OF 1965, WHICH ENABLED MORE AND MORE AFRICAN-AMERICANS TO REGISTER AND VOTE.

New Directions

The NAACP continued to work through the courts to achieve equality. It aimed to change the laws governing capital punishment. Capital punishment is the sentence of death for a crime. It is sometimes called the death penalty. The death penalty is reserved for very serious crimes. However, it was not always applied fairly. Researchers found that African-Americans were more likely than whites to be sentenced to death. The NAACP introduced several legal cases challenging the use of the death penalty. In rulings in 1972 and 1976, the Supreme Court set new standards for the use of the death penalty.

THIS PRISONER, WAITING IN HIS JAIL CELL, WAS SENTENCED TO DIE. THE NAACP HAS CHALLENGED THE USE OF THE DEATH PENALTY.

In 1978, the NAACP started a program for high school students called Academic, Cultural, Technological and Scientific Olympics (ACT-SO). This yearlong program is designed to improve and encourage high academic and cultural achievement among students of color. Students can participate in programs sponsored by NAACP branches in categories such as business, math, music composition, and playwriting. Local winners go to a national competition. In 1987, the Back-to-School/Stay-in-School program was started to reduce the dropout rate among African-American high school students.

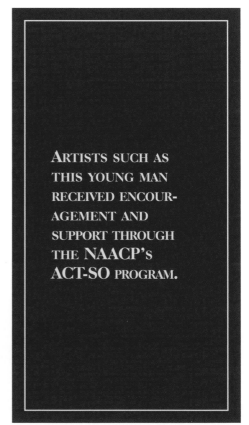

ARTISTS SUCH AS THIS YOUNG MAN RECEIVED ENCOURAGEMENT AND SUPPORT THROUGH THE NAACP'S ACT-SO PROGRAM.

The NAACP also continued to build African-American political power. In the 1980s, the organization registered nearly one million new African-American voters. That number has grown to two million. Still, many African-Americans were concerned that the NAACP was losing its sense of purpose and its importance.

After 16 years as executive director of the NAACP, Dr. Benjamin Hooks retired in 1993, and Rev. Benjamin Chavis replaced him. The next year Chavis was forced to resign after misusing NAACP funds. His actions greatly disappointed the NAACP, but his departure led to a new period of energy. Myrlie Evers-Williams became chair of the NAACP board in 1995. The widow of Medgar Evers, she was important in selecting Kweisi Mfume for NAACP president and chief executive in 1996.

KWEISI MFUME BECAME THE PRESIDENT AND CHIEF EXECUTIVE OF THE NAACP IN 1996.

Mfume was a congressman from Baltimore, Maryland. He improved the NAACP's financial condition and set new goals for the organization that reinforced its commitment to civil rights. He called for increased action in six areas: civil rights, political power, education, economic development, health, and youth outreach. Julian Bond, a civil rights activist who had worked with Dr. King in the 1960s, was elected chair of the NAACP board in 1998.

As it entered a new century, the NAACP continued to work for equality for all Americans. In 2000, the NAACP led a boycott of South Carolina businesses. The boycott was a protest against the flying of the Confederate flag on the state's government buildings. The flag is a symbol of slavery to many African-Americans. The NAACP also signed agreements with the four major television networks to increase diversity in front of and behind the cameras. The group hoped to increase opportunities for people of color in all network operations.

The NAACP continued to work through the courts to end discrimination in different areas. It brought lawsuits against restaurant chains that discriminated against African-Americans. It also settled several historic lawsuits, one involving a national hotel chain and another against the agencies responsible for voting problems in Florida during the 2000 presidential election. These problems had led to many registered voters, especially African-Americans, not being able to vote.

Since the founding of the NAACP in 1909, the organization's activities have helped to change America for the better. In courtrooms as well as on the streets, the people of the NAACP have worked to promote equality and improve the lives of millions of Americans.

TODAY, THE **NAACP** CONTINUES ITS WORK FOR EQUAL RIGHTS. THESE
MEMBERS PROTESTED THE FLYING OF THE **CONFEDERATE** FLAG OVER **SOUTH
CAROLINA'S** GOVERNMENT BUILDINGS.

Timeline

1905	A group of 29 African-Americans founds the Niagara Movement in Fort Erie, Ontario, Canada.
1908	Race riots take place in Springfield, Illinois, on August 14.
1909	The National Negro Committee, which later becomes the NAACP, is founded on February 12.
1910	W. E. B. Du Bois publishes the first issue of the *Crisis* magazine.
1915	The NAACP leads a boycott of *The Birth of a Nation,* a film about the Civil War and the rise of the Ku Klux Klan.
1917	The NAACP works to change government rules to allow African-Americans to serve as officers in the military.
1919	The NAACP issues a report called "30 Years of Lynching in the United States: 1889–1918." NAACP membership grows to around 90,000.
1920	James Weldon Johnson becomes the first African-American executive secretary of the NAACP.
1934	The NAACP hires Charles Hamilton Houston as its first special counsel.
1935	NAACP lawyers win a court battle to admit an African-American student to the University of Maryland.
1938	Thurgood Marshall begins serving as NAACP chief counsel.
1954	The Supreme Court rules that the separate but equal doctrine violates the Constitution.
1955	Rosa Parks is arrested for refusing to give up her bus seat to a white rider. After the Montgomery, Alabama, bus boycott and a NAACP lawsuit, the Supreme Court makes segregation on Alabama buses illegal in 1956.
1960	Members of the NAACP youth council in the South begin protesting segregation at store lunch counters.
1963	The NAACP and other African-American groups organize the historic March on Washington for Jobs and Freedom. More than 250,000 people take part. An NAACP leader named Medgar Evers is murdered in front of his house in Jackson, Mississippi.
1968	To honor African-American actors and actresses, the NAACP establishes the Image Awards.
1970s	The NAACP wages a legal battle against the death penalty.
1978	The NAACP starts a program for youth called Academic, Cultural, Technological and Scientific Olympics (ACT-SO).
1980s	The NAACP leads an African-American voter registration drive.
1987	The NAACP starts the "Back-to-School/Stay-in-School" program to reduce the dropout rate among high school students.
1993	Dr. Benjamin Hooks, NAACP executive director, retires.
1994	Rev. Benjamin Chavis is forced to resign as executive director after misusing NAACP funds.
1995	Myrlie Evers-Williams, the widow of Medgar Evers, becomes chair of the NAACP board.
1996	Kweisi Mfume becomes president and chief executive of the NAACP.
1998	Julian Bond is elected chair of the NAACP board.

Glossary

activist (AK-tih-vist)
An activist is someone who takes direct action for a particular cause. In 1909, activists formed the National Negro Committee, which later became the NAACP.

African-Americans (AF-ri-kehn uh-MER-ih-kehnz)
African-Americans are black Americans whose ancestors came from Africa. Famous African-American W. E. B. Du Bois was the leader of the Niagara Movement.

boycott (BOI-kot)
A boycott is a refusal to buy or use a product or service as a form of protest. The NAACP led a boycott in 1915 against the movie *The Birth of a Nation* because of the way it portrayed African-Americans.

civil rights (SIV-il RITES)
Civil rights are rights that all citizens should have, no matter what their race or background is. The NAACP was founded to fight discrimination and support civil rights.

discriminated (diss-KRIM-uh-NAY-tid)
Being discriminated against is being treated unfairly based on race, sex, or background. Martin Luther King Jr. organized a boycott against the Montgomery bus system, which discriminated against African-Americans.

doctrine (DOK-trin)
A doctrine is a belief or teaching of a group of people. In 1954, the U.S. Supreme Court ruled that the separate but equal doctrine violated the Constitution.

justified (JUHSS-tuh-fyd)
Justified means just or right. "This nation will never stand justified before God until these things are changed," Du Bois wrote in the Niagara Movement's Declaration of Principles.

Ku Klux Klan (KOO kluhks KLAN)
The Ku Klux Klan is a group of secret societies opposed to African-Americans, Jews, and other minorities. Also called the KKK or the Klan, this white hate group operates in the United States and Canada.

lynching (LIN-ching)
Lynching is the taking of a person's life by mob violence, often by hanging. In the 1880s and 1890s, hundreds of African-Americans were killed in lynchings.

racist (RAY-sist)
A racist belief is a belief that one race of people is better than another. The NAACP felt *The Birth of a Nation* portrayed African-Americans in a racist way.

rampage (RAM-payj)
A rampage is a wild outbreak. On August 14, 1908, in Springfield, Illinois, a white mob went on a rampage, burning African-American homes.

riots (RYE-uhtz)
Riots are noisy, violent public disorders. The 1908 riots in Springfield, Illinois, stirred white supporters of the Niagara Movement into action to end racial injustice in the United States.

Glossary

segregation (seg-ruh-GAY-shuhn)
Segregation is the practice of keeping racial groups apart by maintaining separate schools and public facilities. Segregation was widespread in the United States at the start of the 1900s.

sit-ins (SIT-inz)
Sit-ins are a form of protest in which people enter a public place and remain seated for a long period of time. In 1960, members of the NAACP youth council in the South staged sit-ins to protest segregation at lunch counters.

special counsel (SPESH-ul KOUN-suhl)
Special counsel is a lawyer who represents an organization when another lawyer might have a conflict or be biased. In 1934, the NAACP hired Charles Hamilton Houston as its first special counsel.

Index

Further Information

Books

Harris, Jacqueline L. *History and Achievement of the NAACP.* New York: Franklin Watts, 1992.

McKissack, Patricia, and Fredrick McKissack. *Ida B. Wells-Barnett: A Voice against Violence.* Springfield, N.J.: Enslow, 2001.

Paterra, M. Elizabeth. *Kweisi Mfume: Congressman and NAACP Leader.* Springfield, N.J.: Enslow, 2001.

Rowh, Mark. *Thurgood Marshall: Civil Rights Attorney and Supreme Court Justice.* Springfield, N.J.: Enslow, 2002.

Troy, Don. *W. E. B. Du Bois.* Chanhassen, Minn.: The Child's World, 1998.

Web Sites

Visit our homepage for lots of links about the NAACP:

http://www.childsworld.com/links.html

Note to Parents, Teachers, and Librarians:
We routinely verify our Web links to make sure they're safe,
active sites—so encourage your readers to check them out!

About the Author

Andrew Santella is the author of a number of nonfiction books for young readers. He also writes regularly for publications ranging from the *New York Times Book Review* to *GQ.* He is a graduate of Loyola University in Chicago.